Meet Tom

An Interview with

MW00463044

Illustrated by Mike Dammer   **Photography by Jon Reed**

Celebration Press
An Imprint of Pearson Learning

Who is Tom Paxton?

I am a folk singer, songwriter, and author. My songs and books are about children, grown-ups, animals, sports, and nature.

When did you begin to play music?

When I was nine, I visited a ranch in
Arizona. I heard a real cowboy sing a
wonderful, funny song. After that, I
got my own guitar and started
singing and writing.

Why did you start
to write books
for kids?

I was already writing songs for kids.
I thought writing books for kids
would be just as much fun.

How do you think of ideas
for your books and songs?

I sit down and think and think.
If an idea pops into my head,
I write it down right away.
Ideas can be slippery.

Who is your favorite character?

Engelbert the Elephant is my
favorite character. I love the sound of
his name. He is also a little slow and
clumsy, just like I am sometimes.

What do you do when you're
stuck for ideas?

I tap my fingers and feet and just
start writing! If I don't get any good
ideas, I have something to eat.
Snacking always works for me.

What kinds of things
do you like to read?

When I was a kid, I read every book
I could find about cowboys, horses,
dogs, and nature. Now I love reading
books about baseball.

Dear Readers,

All my life I have loved to read books. I think this is why I began to write books. The same thing may happen with you. What a great thought! I would love to read the books you write, so I hope you begin soon. Good reading! Good writing!

Your friend,

Tom Payton